Pizza Success Secrets

The 7 Things You Must Do To Have A Highly Profitable Pizza Business

Paul Baker

Pizza Success Secrets

The 7 Things You Must Do To Have A Highly Profitable Pizza Business

© 2014 Paul Baker

Limit of Liability/Disclaimer of Warranty: While the author and publisher have used their best efforts in preparing this book, they make no representation or warranties regarding the accuracy or completeness of the contents of this book. The author and publisher specifically disclaim any implied warranties of merchantability or fitness for a particular purpose, and makes no guarantees whatsoever that you will achieve any particular result. Any case studies presented herein do not necessarily represent what you should expect to achieve since business success depends on a variety of factors. We believe all case studies and results presented herein are true and accurate, but we have not audited the results. The advice and strategies contained in this book may not even be suitable for your situation, and you should consult your own advisors as appropriate. The author and publisher shall not be held liable for any loss of profit or any other commercial damages included but not limited to special, incidental, consequential, or other damages. The fact that on organization or website is referred to in this work as a citation and/or a potential source of information does not mean does not mean that the author or publisher endorses the information the organization or website may provide or the recommendations it may make. Further, readers should be aware that Internet websites listed in this book may have changed or disappeared after this book was written.

Earning Disclaimer: The author does not believe in get rich quick programs, all human progress and accomplishment takes hard work. As stipulated by law, we cannot and do not make any guarantees about your ability to get results or earn any money with our ideas, information, tools or strategies. It takes hard work to succeed in any type of business. In fact it takes hard work to succeed at anything in life. Just try entering a mixed martial arts competition without putting in any training, practice or hard work and see how that goes. Nothing in this book, or any of our websites is a promise or guarantee of results or future earnings and we do not offer any legal, medical, tax, or other professional advice. Any financial numbers referenced in this book or any of our websites are simply estimates or projections and should not be considered exact, actual or as a promise of future earnings, all numbers are for illustrative purposes only.

Table of contents

Preface

After being in the pizza business for over 14 years, I am convinced that over 90% of the pizza restaurants that are scraping by from day to day, are letting no less than $100,000 per year in profits either walk out the door with their customers or losing it to any of the other proverbial money sucking black holes that exist in our industry.

Think about it, $100,000 per year. That money could be going directly into your pockets, providing you and your family with a better life style. Instead, all that money seems to... disappear. Or worse yet, most pizzeria owners don't even realize it's slipping through their fingers. But the money is there, hiding waiting to be discovered like a lost treasure. This book is your treasure map to the small fortune that's hiding inside your pizzeria. It's your job to follow the map.

When I originally begin putting this book together, I had the full intention of it being another marketing and sales building book. However, that changed when I sat down to talk with a woman named Tommie about her pizzeria. She honestly had one of the best tasting pizzas I had ever eaten, but her sales were horrible, and she was losing money left and right. Within 15 minutes of talking with her, and taking a walk through her pizzeria, I had identified three things that she was not doing that had the potential of sucking out $20,000 per year out of her pocket.

Tommie wasn't the first pizzeria owner I've talked with that was neglecting doing these three things, so as we walked through her pizzeria in the back of my mind I'm thinking "Here we go again, she's neglecting the same things that almost everyone else does."

At this point, something "clicked" and I realized that most pizzeria owners that I consult or talk with are all not doing these three things. By not doing these three things, it wouldn't matter if I helped her double or triple her sales, she would simple bleed most the profit out.

After my conversation with Tommie, I began looking at all the things that I've found normally occur in struggling pizza restaurants. What I discovered is that there are 7 predominate things that continually rear their ugly heads in our industry. You may or may not be doing all 7, but just ignoring or not doing one or two can be detrimental to your profits. I would even go so far as to say that a majority of the pizza shop failures that occur are a result of ignoring these 7 things.

Don't simply take my word for it. Do this simple test. Go to Craigslist and find some pizzerias for sale. Most of the time, the pizzerias for sale on Craigslist are listed by struggling, broke, and desperate owners trying to dump their stores before they are forced to close their doors, and depending on what part of the country you're in, there's usually a lot of them listed. Call up these owners and begin asking them about their operations. Go through the list of the 7 things in this book. You'll find in over 90% of the cases, most if not all of these 7 things are being ignored.

Combine not doing (or not knowing about) these 7 things with the "myth" that all you need to operate a successful pizzeria (or any restaurant for that matter) is good service, good food, and low prices and you have the perfect recipe for financial disaster. I actually saw an article posted called "How to have a successful pizza restaurant" that said you were practically guaranteed success if you had great food, great service and the lowest prices. Dumb! Dumb! Dumb!

This kind of advice is the most expensive that you could ever receive. God knows how many people have put up their homes as collateral or taken out their life savings to open a restaurant on this bad advice only to find they are bankrupt and in financial ruin within two years. I remember myself when I bought my store having a similar experience.

There we were in the dining room, my wife, myself, and the "bigwigs" of the franchise system we were about to buy into. I had seen the store sales for the previous year and they were pretty dismal. I asked the bigwig what it would take to get sales up. He immediately spit out the classic "Great food, great service, and competitive pricing" line. So after signing on the dotted line, I dropped prices, started putting a little bit more toppings on the pizzas to make them better and provided the best possible service I was capable of. Four months later two things had happened...

...jack and shit.

Sales didn't go up a bit, profit was something I only dreamed of, and my wife was about to kill me for "getting us into this stupid business".

Fortunately, things turned out ok for us, but that's not always the case for a lot of other pizzeria owners out there. Most will eventually end up having to close their doors, being unable to make payroll or rent. Still others may be able to keep their head above water for several years, but never be able to bring in a good solid income.

If you're one of those owners who are about to "go under" then this book could be the life preserver that allows you to grab that bottom rung and start pulling yourself out of the pool of financial distress.

Even if you think you're doing "ok" with your pizza business and showing a profit, this book will help you find the hidden money that is "falling through the cracks." And keep this in mind, even if you are currently doing solid sales with your pizzeria, no one is immune to the "next big disaster" that everyone in business faces on a daily basis.

This could be anything from a new competitor moving in next door to the State deciding to reroute the highway from in front of your business to a mile away, or even just a simple repaving job that takes six months to complete which kills off all your traffic (I've personally seen all these scenarios). If this happens your chances of surviving greatly increases if you're running a competent, lean business that maximizes every dollar and customer that comes in.

How To Get The
Most From This Book

Chapter 1

I n most cases when reading any business, nonfiction, or how-to book, the author saves the best "tip" or "strategy" for last, encouraging you to read through the entire book.

I don't want you to do that. I've purposely put what I consider the most valuable and important thing at the very front of the book, which is raising your prices. After reading this, I want you to put the book down and immediately go and implement. After, and only after you have done this should you finish reading this book. After finishing this book, begin implementing any of the other six things that you are not already doing in your store.

In each section of this book, if applicable, I will show you how much money you are potentially losing or could be making. To keep the math as simple as possible we will be using a sales average of $25,000 per month. Your sales might be higher or lower, just adjust the math for what your sales are in your store.

I've also included a bonus chapter. While this chapter is not one of the seven things that we will cover in this book, it is nonetheless just as important, if not more so than the other chapters in this book. It covers the "million dollar question" that you must answer. And I don't use "million dollar" lightly. Being able to answer this question quite literally could make the difference between you have a million dollar pizzeria or a struggling business that seems to choke the life out of you at every turn.

I urge you to carefully read this chapter several times until you really grasp the concept and can answer the million dollar question for yourself.

Raise Your Prices

Chapter 2

Here is the fastest, easiest, and most efficient way to add sales revenue to your business literally overnight. It's simply to raise your prices.

You probably just read that first paragraph and thought to yourself "Well there's a blinding flash of the obvious." You can call it obvious if you like, but try explaining why almost every pizzeria owner out there is afraid to raise their prices. I see it every time I suggest to a client that they need to raise their prices. Beads of sweat start forming on their brow, their hands go clammy and they blurt out the usual reply of "I can't raise my prices, all my customers will leave and buy from my competitors."

Admittedly, there is a psychological barrier to raising prices, however, that barrier is in the mind of the business owner, not the customer! Most pizzeria owners falsely believe that if they raise their prices higher than their competitors, people will stop buying from them. This fear couldn't be further from the truth. There have been numerous studies done, and they all show that people rarely buy on price, and actually, price is one of the least important things when customers are making a decision of who to buy from.

I know a lot of people will point to Wal-Mart and say see... they compete on price, and look how successful they are. And you're right, right now Wal-Mart is very successful because of their prices, but I would venture to say that might not be the case within the next 20 years.

Look back at the other big retail stores that have tried to use price as their main buying point to customers. There was Montgomery Ward, they are no longer in business, there was Sears, they almost went bankrupt and just managed to survive, and right before Wal-Mart began taking the lead as price king, there was K-Mart.

So if a new competitor was to arise tomorrow, and have all their merchandise at half the price that Wal-Mart does, do you think Wal-Mart would still be able to hold on to as many sales as they have now? Maybe, maybe not. But see how risky using low prices are to your business? You might be the lowest price one day, and the next day you're not. So what do you use for your slogan then? Lowest price some days?

If everyone bought just on price, we would all be driving around in tiny cheap cars, and living in inexpensive one bedroom apartments. Engagement rings would be imitation gold with fake diamonds, and no one would be wearing name brand clothes.

You've probably heard the passage from the Bible… "if you live by the sword, you die by the sword" well, if you live by price, you will die by price. If you're trying to compete with the big chain stores based on price alone, you're going to die a slow painful death.

I've seen the big chain stores drop prices so low that you would swear that they were losing money with each sale they make. And there's a really good possibility that they are.

But by dropping prices that low, and having the deep pockets that they do it's simply a matter of time before the small pizza shops go under trying to compete with them based on price. This is a tactic that if you keep your eyes peeled you will see happen in a lot of businesses where there are large chains. They simply move into a new area, drop prices so low that the little guys go out of business, then bring their prices back up after they have eliminated their competition.

Think this doesn't ever happen? Watch the next time a large chain store opens up in your neighborhood. They'll leave their prices high when they first open because everyone will be trying them out because they are new in town.

But then, they will drop prices to where they are breaking even, or even taking a small loss, to get all the business in the area. And if this happens in your neighborhood, there's no way you can drop your prices with them and think you can wait them out.

It's simply a matter of attrition. They have the cash to take a loss for several years if needed. You probably have the cash to last a few months if you're lucky.

When you raise your prices, one of three things are going to happen. Your sales will go up, your sales will go down, or your sales will stay the same.

Your sales will go up:
As incredible as this may sound, there is a possibility that your sales will actually go up when you raise your prices. This is due to price psychology.

If you wanted to go out and purchase the best watch on the market, what's the first thing you would look at? Price! Its human nature, it's programmed into us. If we want the best of anything, the first that we look at is price.

Take two pizzas from two different stores. Both stores order their food supplies from the same distributor. One charges $19.99 for a large pizza, the other charges $5.99 for basically the same pizza.

If you were going to take someone that you had just started dating out for pizza, which pizza would you buy for them? If you bought them the $5.99 pizza, you would run a risk of being thought of as cheap, even though both pizzas are made the same, the one that is selling for $5.99 has a perceived worth of only $5.99!

Can you see where this is going? You're the one who decides how your pizza is perceived based on the price that you put on it.

Now you obviously can't buy the cheapest ingredients possible, then skimp on the cheese and toppings and charge a high price for it and have people not find you out.

Here's a great example of the perceived value of an item based on price. Women's underwear.

You can go to almost any department store and get a basic cotton pair of underwear for about $1.34 per pair. These have a really low perceived value. Now this same pair of cotton underwear will cost you over $5.00 per pair at Victoria's Secret. These are perceived as having a little bit more value than the $1.34 pair, however their both made out of the exact same material.

Let's go even further. Above the Victoria's Secret underwear, there's the Australian Wicked Weasel brand panty that sells for $15.46 each. That's over 1000% higher than the basic pair you can get out of a retail or department store! Same cotton panty as the other two, but a much higher perceived value.

And if that difference in price doesn't blow your mind, for the same basic item, you can go to www.nancymeyer.com and check out the Carine Gilson Silk and Lace Shorty for the everyday low price of only $448.00! Granted, it's not made out of cotton like the other pairs, but it's not plated in gold either, it's just a lace panty!

Same basic item, huge difference in perceived value. What if Nancy Meyer had listed the price on their panty at $19.99 each instead of the $448? You wouldn't have jumped online as soon as you read about them and checked them out would you?

Same thing with your pizza. Most people think that the more expensive something is, the better it is, so your marketplace will end up taking you at your own appraisal.

Raising prices can actually end up increasing your sales.

Your sales will go down:
The other thing that can happen is that your sales go down. More than likely, you will have a few of the bottom feeding coupon clippers that will get mad if you raise prices and jump ship.

These are the customers you probably don't want anyway, and probably would have bailed to one of your competitors the first time they got a coupon in the mail for $2.00 off a large pizza.

The fact of the matter is that if you just raised your prices by a tiny 10%, you could lose up to 10% of your customers, and still have almost the same amount of sales as you did before raising your prices.

This means that if you had 5000 customers in your data base, you could lose 500 of them because of the 10% price increase, but do you really think that 500 of your customers would leave you because of such a small increase?

When I raised prices by a buck per pizza, I had only two people complain about it, no one else even blinked when we told them their totals. It's like they didn't even realize what the price of the pizza was before the price increase. Actually, let's take a quick quiz and see if we know how much other business charge for their products.

How much does a gallon of milk cost at your local grocery store? What about a box of laundry detergent at your local retailer? How much is Burger King charging for a large milkshake? How about your local burger restaurant, how much do they get for one of their hamburgers?

Could you name the exact price off the top of your head for any of those items? Probably not. That's because most people don't know what your prices are, and if you make tiny increments, they're not going to notice them.

Now you can't make a jump from $9.99 to $15.99 and think no one will notice, but most people won't notice you going from $9.99 to $10.99.

Your sales will stay the same:

This is most likely what will happen when you raise your prices. Most people won't even notice the price increase, and will go about doing business with you as normal.

If you have just raised your sales by 10%, and your sales stay the same, you have just added a huge amount of money to your bottom line. How much? Let's take a look.

To keep the numbers simple, let's say you have 1000 regular customers, ordering once per month, with an average ticket of $25.00

1000 customers x $25.00 = $25,000 per month

Now by raising prices only 10%, our average order now becomes $27.50 per month.

1000 customers x 27.50 = $27,500 per month

That's an instant $2500 profit every month! That's an additional $30,000 in profit every year! What could you do with an extra $30,000 every year in practically free money?

See how profitable this can be? You absolutely need to do this. Implement this as soon as you get done reading this chapter, it's that important to your bottom line.

It's strange to me when I see someone buy an existing business and the first thing they do is drop the prices that the previous owner had. I've seen this firsthand when I first put my store up for sale.

I had a woman who was very interested in purchasing my store and had flown down from the state of Washington to take a look at the store and possibly sign contracts for the sale.

While we were sitting down at lunch, discussing terms and such, I asked her how she planned on marketing the store. Very first words out of her mouth were…. "I'm going to cut prices".

So here is a woman who has done (as far as I know) no real market research on the area. Didn't ask any customers if they thought the prices were too high. And didn't have any other real marketing plan other than cutting prices!

At the end of the day, she couldn't decide if she wanted to sign an agreement and put money down on the store. Even though I wanted to sell my store, I told her that if she wasn't 100% sure, then she shouldn't buy. If she had purchased the store, she was going to cut prices by $2.00 per pizza. That's like taking a job and telling your boss… I would much rather work for $9.00 per hour than $19.00 per hour. It's stealing out of your own pocket.

Using Social Media
Instead of Direct Mail

Chapter 3

Before we get started in this section, I would like to run you through a brief exercise. Don't worry, I promise you it won't take long. Go grab yourself a pencil and paper. Now, I want you to write down the number of orders or sales that you've positively, without a doubt made from your Facebook, Twitter, or other social media advertising efforts. Don't guess, or write down a number that you "think" might be close to the correct number. Really think about this. Ok... now set that paper aside and we'll come back to it in a minute.

Now, remember at the beginning of this book when I told you to call some pizzerias listed on Craigslist and ask them about the things in this book? You do? Great! Because here is one of the questions I want you to ask them...

"What are you currently doing for advertising?"

When you ask them this question, you're almost always going to get one of two answers. The first is "We use word of mouth advertising." Translated that means "We don't do shit." The second answer your likely to get is "We advertise on Facebook."

Ok... now reach over to that paper you had just a minute ago and look at the number of sales that you know without a shadow of doubt came from your Facebook or other social media advertising. It's probably pretty depressing – huh.

I'm NOT telling you to stop using Facebook or Twitter to advertise and market your pizzeria on. In fact – I encourage you to continue to advertise with social media. Here's where the problem lies though. In almost every failing pizzeria that I encounter, their primary form of marketing their business is Facebook.

These pizzeria owners seem to think that if they have a lot of "likes" on their Facebook page then their Facebook advertising is working. The late copywriting legend Gary Halbert said it best. He had numerous internet marketers telling him how great their website was doing and how many "hits" per day they were getting. Gary asked them one simple question: "How many sales have you made?" The usual answer was none yet, or just a few. Gary then told these internet marketers that "hits" stands for How Idiots Track Success! He's absolutely right. It doesn't matter how many hits or likes you get on your Facebook page, the only "like" that really matters is the one that comes into your store and buys something!

You absolutely must understand that social media, compared to other forms of advertising… sucks. And to rely on it as your primary source of marketing and advertising is setting yourself up for disaster.

Gallup did an unbiased poll in June of 2014. That poll revealed that 63% of consumers are NOT influenced by social media regarding their buying choices, and only 5% claim that social media has a significant impact on their buying decisions. Once again… I'm not saying that you shouldn't use social media, but I am telling you to avoid the "social media hype" and not to fall victim to the false belief that social media has replaced other marketing and advertising vehicles.

If you happen to be that one in 1000 person that is making a killing using social media in your pizzeria I'm extremely happy for you, (and please contact me and let me know how you're doing it) but keep this in mind. At any time Facebook could completely change the rules and everything that you're doing could come to a screeching halt. And don't believe for a second that this couldn't happen.

Just a few years ago there we're companies making millions off of search engine advertising on Google. One day out of the blue, Google changed all the rules. They didn't tell anyone how or why they changed them, they just did it. Those companies making millions had their revenue streams dry up literally overnight.

So what do I recommend using for advertising? I recommend using direct mail as one of your primary forms of advertising. Hold on you say… direct mail is outdated and expensive and not as "hip" as social media. Well… you right about one of the three. Direct mail might not be as "hip" as social media, but if used correctly, it's certainly is not expensive and not nearly as outdated as you might think.

Direct mail is still a multi-billion dollar a year business. The gigantic Fortune 500 companies use it to turn enormous profits every year. Look at your mail, is there a day or week that goes by that you don't get a piece of mail from Lowes, Wal-mart, Apple or from any of the large banks issuing credit cards? And guess what… even the tech giant Google sends out direct mail to its potential prospects.

Warning: I'm NOT telling you to copy what these large companies are doing with their direct mail. You being a small business will have different needs and goals than what these big companies do. The point is, direct mails works if you use the right format for your business.

At a glance, direct mail might look expensive, but let's take a closer look. In my pizzeria I sent out direct mail sales letters to the small market of 6,300 households in my zip code. Usually I would average about a 5% response on these letters (315 redeemed). Depending on the letter and time of year the response could go as high as 8% and as low as 3%. I never had a response lower than 3% on a direct mail letter campaign. At the time, each one of these mail campaigns would cost me around $2100 to mail out.

Depending on the offer, the average sale on these direct mail letters was $19.50 per order, resulting in around $6142.50 in sales. Not a bad return on a $2100 investment. Do you know of very many stocks you can purchase and get that kind of return in that amount of time? I doubt it. But let's go a step further with this.

As a result of these direct mail campaigns, I averaged around 100 new customers every month. On average, I could convert 8 of those to becoming regular customers. My regular customers purchased on average twice per month with and average ticket of $18.00

So every month I was adding eight people to my customer base that was each spending $36 per month (sometimes more).

$36.00 x 8 customers = $288 per month

Now at the end of 12 months if I've maintained my 8 person per month average, I now have an additional 96 regular customers in my data base spending $36 per month with me.

$36 x 96 customers = $3,456 per month
$3,456 per month x 12 months = $41,472 per year

And these numbers can continue to compound with additional direct mail that keeps your customers coming back more often and that gets them to spend more.

As you can see, direct mail can be very lucrative to your bottom line. It's folly to only rely of Facebook because it appears to be a free form of advertising. And looking at these numbers, which actually costs you more? The direct mail letter campaign that brings in 315 orders, or the Facebook ad that brings in two or three orders?

I just want to reiterate again that I'm not telling you to stop using social media. I'm only telling you to not use it as your only form of advertising because it's free. Use it in conjunction with direct mail and you will see much better results. Here's a great example of how you could use direct mail letters and Facebook to create an extremely powerful marketing campaign.

After dropping off your letters at the post office or mailing house, jump on your Facebook account and post a message letting everyone know that you have put a letter in the mail for them and they should be receiving it in the next day or two.

Don't tell them anything else. Don't elaborate on the letter and don't tell them anything about what it will say, just leave the message at that. What this does is create enormous curiosity about what the letter is about. So now when your letter arrives in the mail, your customer is actively looking for it and expecting it, unlike all the other advertisements that show up in their mailbox on a daily basis.

Even if you can't afford to do big mass mailings to your entire town or service area, at the very least do small, micro targeted mailings to your current best customers.

Eventually someone will "crack the code" on how to use social media with pizza restaurants and get big and fast returns with it, but until then you need to look at social media as a long term strategy and not as something that you can quickly build your pizzeria on by itself.

Portion Control

Chapter 4

It still surprises me after all these years how many pizzerias refuse to use portion control in their stores. I've heard almost every excuse imaginable from "my employees refuse to do it" to "It slows down production" and some even try to make it sound like they are artists with the "we only free throw our toppings" line of crap.

As far as employees – if they refuse to use portion control fire their stupid ass. And if you want to be artistic, just remember that the world is full of starving artists for a reason.

The fact of the matter is... not weighing and counting your toppings and using portion control is stupid. You don't want to be stupid do you?

There are two primary reasons why you want to always use portion control. The first, and most obvious, is money. The amount of money that can walk out of your pizzeria in the form of extra toppings thrown on a pizza can be enormous. Let's look at our pizzeria that's doing $25,000 per month in sales. If they are selling 2500 14 inch pizzas per month and using 8oz of cheese per pizza at $2.75 per pound then it's costing them $1.38 per pizza in cheese costs.

Now let's say that little Johnny the cook free throws cheese on every pizza. Because he's been there for several years he gets pretty close to 8oz of cheese every time and only misses by 2oz. At the end of the month, just 2oz of extra cheese going on those 2500 pizzas is costing you an additional $862.25 or $10,350 per year.

And that's if he only adds two additional ounces extra per pizza. The reality is he's probably throwing closer to three extra ounces per pizza. Keep in mind also we're only talking about cheese right now, this isn't taking into consideration that little Johnny is probably throwing on extra pepperoni, ham, sausage, mushrooms, etc…. If you're running any kind of decent sales volume at all and not using portion control you're flushing huge sums of money down the toilet every year.

Go ahead and take a $100 dollar bill out of your wallet, tear it up into little pieces as you're standing over the toilet bowl. Let it flutter into the water and watch it as it swirls around the bowl a few times and is then gone forever. Let that feeling settle into your gut because that's exactly what you're doing every time you neglect portion control.

I always used portion control on every aspect of making a pizza. From weighing the dough balls to measuring out the sauce to counting the pepperonis. I had extensive charts that my employees could look at for each size pizza and know exactly how much of each ingredient to use.

If you don't currently have charts for your employees, get some made as soon as possible. You can't expect your employees to memorize the weights and counts for every size pizza and topping. Have charts plastered right in front of their faces so no excuses can be made for failing to use portion control.

If you don't already have charts and are not sure how much of each topping should be used on your pizza, the figure 4:1 chart is a good starting point. Adjust the topping amounts until you get your pizzas how you want them. Once you have them, make your charts and have your employees build off of those charts.

Whenever I hired someone, I always had them read and sign a form explaining that if they were ever caught "free throwing" toppings and not using portion control, the would be fired. There were no second chances or excuses and I only had to fire someone for this twice in 10 years.

Figure 4:1

14 Inch Pizza	1 Topping	2X Topping	3X Topping
Cheese	8 ounces	8 ounces	8 ounces
Pepperoni	40 count	24 count	18 count
Canadian Bacon	40 count	24 count	18 count
Mushrooms	5 ounces	3 ounces	1.5 ounces
Green Peppers	5 ounces	2 ounces	1.5 ounces
Onions	5 ounces	2 ounces	1.5 ounces
Pork Sausage	8 ounces	5 ounces	3 ounces
Hamburger	8 ounces	5 ounces	3 ounces
Italian Sausage	6 ounces	4 ounces	2 ounces
Bacon	5 ounces	3 ounces	2 ounces
Chicken	5 ounces	3 ounces	2 ounces

The second reason you should use portion control is for consistency. Your customers want your product to be consistent. They don't want to be surprised by different amounts of toppings each time they come in. In almost 10 years, I never had a complaint that the last time someone got a pizza from me it had more toppings on it, and that's because each pizza was made exactly the same.

Look at McDonalds. Do they have a great product? Nope, it's basically a crappy meat product squeezed between two buns with a small glop of ketchup, a small squirt of mustard, one single pickle in the middle and something that I think is supposed to be tiny chopped up onions (I still haven't figured out exactly what that is yet). It's by no means what anyone would consider a great burger. However, when you order one you know exactly what you're going to get. If you were to order one hamburger per day for the next month, all 30 of those hamburgers are going to be exactly the same. Could someone say the same thing about your pizza if they ordered every day? Would they all be exactly the same?

Would you continue to go to your barber or hair stylist if each time you went you weren't sure exactly what kind of haircut you would be getting? People want consistency in what they buy. The only way your pizzas will be consistent is by using portion control.

Having A
Point Of Sale System

Chapter 5

I would never consider going into the pizza business or any kind of restaurant business without a Point of Sale system. Not having one is akin to trying to fly an airplane without instruments. Yes it can be done, but the chances of you safely reaching your destination are greatly diminished. We've all heard the horror stories of pilots losing their instruments at night and having to fly by instinct. Some with years of experience under their belts make it safely, others don't.

It's alarming how many pizzeria owners will jump into this business risking sometimes large sums of capital and think they can skimp when it comes to a POS system. They seem to think that just having a basic cash register will suffice. They couldn't be further from the truth. Let's look at all the reasons why you must have a POS system for your pizzeria.

Employee Theft:

The National Restaurant Association attributes 30 percent of all restaurant failures to employee theft. Read that statement again. That's not saying that 30% of restaurants have theft – that's saying that 30% of the restaurants that are forced to close their doors have to do so as a result of theft. If you really don't think it's happening in your pizzeria, you're being naive.

While there's no way to prevent 100% of the theft that happens, a POS system will help prevent a lot of it from taking place. On a daily basis, I would look at the "voided" tickets for the day. On one occasion my manager found seven voided tickets from lunch. The POS system told us who voided them, what time they were voided and the amount of each ticket and all of the customer's information. I called each of the customers and told them that I was just checking up to see why they cancelled their orders earlier that day to see if there was some aspect of our operation and customer service that we could improve on. All seven customers said that they had picked up their order and paid for it at the register.

This girl, if we would have had a regular cash register and written orders down on paper tickets, might have given herself a "bonus" and made off with over $100 that day in voided sales.

Here's another example. My brother took over a small hamburger stand that had been in his wife's family for generations. This place was a little cash cow as it was the only hamburger place in town. They did everything the old fashioned way, wrote orders on tickets and had cash registers that anyone could get into at any time. He complained to me that at the end of the night, the cash never settled out with what his register tapes said.

When I asked him how much the difference was he told me some nights it might be $100 bucks short, sometimes $300 or $400! I convinced him to purchase a used POS system for $3000 bucks. Guess what, the register tapes begin settling correctly, sales went up, and food cost went down. The amount of cash and free food walking out of the place was unbelievable.

Customer Cultivation:
Another reason to have a POS is for customer cultivation. Your current customers are an absolute gold mine if you work them right.

I've noticed that a lot of pizzerias that do have a POS system, once they get a name, address and phone number don't do anything with the information. They act like the only reason to have the POS is so that their employees don't have to reenter in the customer's information each time they order. While this is one of the perks of having a POS, not working your customer list is like driving a Ferrari but never taking it out of first gear.

I want you to imagine for a minute that you're a rancher back in the days of the Wild West. You're primary source of food and income is your herd. The larger your herd is, the bigger your income is. Would you not try to make your herd as large as you possibly could? If some of your herd wandered off would you not go out and look for them and bring them back?

Your customer base is your herd. And when you don't work it and care for it, your customers end up wandering off to your competitors taking your sales with them. By not having a POS, or not using your current one to track and retain customers, you're essentially putting your herd in a pasture with no fences to keep them in. Hoping that a few new ones will show up so your herd will get a little bigger, then praying that they don't wander off. And when they do wander off… you have absolutely no idea which ones have disappeared, when they disappeared, or where they went.

Are you starting to see why a POS system is important? It's the fence that keeps your herd from wandering off.

There's a misguided assumption that you need as many new customers as you can get. I say this is misguided because while you do need a steady stream of new customers, it's actually costing you more to get new customers than it would to get your current customers to spend with you again. On average, it can cost up to five times as much to get a new customer to order than it would to get someone who has already ordered from you to order again.

Think about it. If it costs you $1 to get a current customer to buy a $10 pizza from you or $5 to get a new customer to buy a $10 pizza from you, where is your advertising dollar better spent?

What most pizzerias do is spend the $5 to get the new customer. Then, after spending that $5... they ignore the new customer they just got! Remember in the previous chapter when I told you that my direct mail letters would get an average of 5% response and I would usually ad an additional 100 new customers to my "herd"? These letters were mailed to the surrounding zip code with obviously a very good response.

However, once someone had purchased from me and become part of my herd, I could send sales letters to them and get over a 20% response. Let's look at the math again.

If I mail out 1000 letters at .60 cost per letter to people who are not current customers, I can expect to get 50 orders at an average order of $19.50 each, resulting in a profit of $375 after subtracting the cost to mail the letters of $600.

50 orders x $19.50 = $975 sales
$975 sales - $600 letters cost = $375

A $375 dollar profit might not look like a lot, but remember that if just one or two of those 50 orders becomes a regular customer you could easily double or triple that $375 over the next 12 months.

Now if I mail 1000 letters to the customers already in my data base I can expect 200 orders at $19.50 each. So now I'm looking at spending the same $600 to mail the letters, but getting a $3,300 return in sales after mailing costs.

200 orders x 19.50 = $3,900
$3,900 sales - $600 letter cost = $3,300

So which do you think you should be doing more of? Working on your existing herd, or beating the bushes for new customers? Without a POS to capture your customers contact information and track their buying habits you'll never truly be able to reach your profit potential.

Labor Management:
Another reason to have a POS is for labor management. Without one, you're missing the up to the minute stats on what your sales to labor ratio is. The normal routine for someone not using a POS for labor control is for them to write out the weekly schedule based on how many people they'll think they need that week based on what they're guessing sales might be. Then when it comes time to do payroll, they add up how much their labor is and how much they did in sales and "pray" that they don't overshoot their targeted labor percentage.

Using a POS to track your labor can save you a lot of money every month by simply being able to "tweak" the times that your employees are allowed to clock in or leave. Let's use our 25,000 per month example store again and see how much we're losing each month by not having a POS for our labor control.

If our targeted labor percentage is 25% of sales, then our monthly payroll will be $6,250. If you miss your target by only 5% you've just raised your monthly payroll to $7,500.

That's an additional $1,250 out of your pocket at the end of the month or $15,000 per year. And keep in mind that the higher your payroll is, the more you pay in taxes and workers compensation insurance.

After you begin using a POS to track your labor percentage hourly, you can begin to adjust your schedule based on what you now know your sales and labor percentage is in real time.

On average, if I really paid attention I could cut my labor down by 3%. All my staff knew that our target was 25% labor and they all could check the POS at any time to see what it was currently. If the labor was high they knew to send someone home early or to have someone come in 30 minutes or an hour later than their scheduled shift. So if you used your POS and tweaked your scheduling to cut 3% off your target, then you could be saving $750 per month or $9000 per year.

Another way a POS can save you a lot of money on your labor is by tracking how long your delivery drivers are on the road. Check with you workers compensation insurance carrier on this as different carriers probably have different policies, but I was able to record the actual time my delivery drivers were on the road delivering pizzas and paying the higher workers compensation rate only for those hours on the road. The rest of the time the drivers were inside folding boxes, washing dishes or answering phones was billed at the lower "less risk" rate that my in store employees were at.

If I didn't have a POS to prove actual "on the road" times, I could have been charged a lot more for my workers compensation insurance policy. Once again, check with your insurance carrier to see what their policy is on doing this.

Accounting:

One of the things I came to love about my POS was the ability to quickly print out everything for my accountant. When it was time to turn in payroll, it took me 15 seconds to print everyone's time out. At the end of the month I could print out everything my accountant needed to do taxes in less than 30 seconds. These two features can help keep you organized and save time. How much is your time worth?

Customer Retention

Chapter 6

H ave you ever wondered why your customers stop ordering from you? Isn't it confusing and frustrating when they tell you they really love your pizza but then don't come back and order again for weeks or months?

Well I'm about to let you in on the dirty little secret as to why your customers stop ordering from you. It's not because they don't like your pizza. It's not because you gave them lousy service (although this could be an issue if you are not on top of your game). Nope – the real reason your customers stop ordering from you is... They forget!

As simple as this might seem, it's the primary reason why your customers stop ordering from you. They simply forget about you. With all the crazy and hectic things going on in today's society, ordering a pizza from you is definitely not going to be one of the first things they think of when they get up in the morning. When a customer forgets to order from you, or hasn't ordered in a while, they're what's known as a "lazy customer".

Lazy customer is the term used for customers who haven't ordered in 30, 60 or 90 days. Your lazy customer program is the safety net that will catch any customers that may potentially be leaving your herd.

There are two ways that you can try to reactivate a lazy customer. The first is to use the 30, 60, 90 day program. Basically what will happen is at 30 days, you'll send out a reminder to the customer with some low cost free item to get them to come back in. I would usually do the free breadstick offer.

At 60 days, if the customer still hasn't ordered, I would up the offer, and give them a free calizone, which was a nine dollar value, or a free breadstick and 2liter for ordering.

At 90 days, I would send them a letter for a free large pizza in a last desperate attempt to keep them in my herd of active customers. When they hit this 90 day mark, you need to be concerned.

Some customers might have moved off. Some might have lost their jobs. Still others might have been swayed by a coupon from your competitor for a cheap pizza deal.

Whatever the reason, you have to try to get them back.

When the customers that hit the 90 days would come in to redeem their free pizza letter that I sent them, I would make sure that my staff or myself would ask them why they hadn't ordered in so long.

This is key, because you need to know what the reason is behind their long delay in ordering. If a lot of the 90 day customers started telling you that one of your staff members didn't make them feel welcome, then there's a problem that needs to be resolved.

I found that most of the time, the customer won't tell you that their buying from one of your competitors unless something happened that made them mad and resulted in them not coming back.

I know that one time, a lady named Linda redeemed her free pizza, and when asked about why she hadn't been back in so long, she straight up told us that her deliveries were taking over 50 minutes the last three times she had ordered, and didn't want to have to keep waiting that long.

Her telling us this, was worth every penny it cost me to give her that free pizza.

When we reviewed our drivers delivery times for the past month, we noticed that two of our drivers were taking almost 13 minutes longer per delivery than all the other drivers, and these were not new delivery drivers.

This was a problem that we quickly fixed.

So we have the 30, 60, 90 day program. The other way we can catch lazy customers is to just use a 45 and 90 day program.

After using the 30, 60, 90 day program for almost four years, I found that just by using the 45 and 90 day program, you would still keep and reactivate the same number of customers, and it was a lot less work.

The offer at 45 days was the same offer I used at 60 days, and I still had about the same number of customers hit the 90 day mark. So I would recommend just doing the 45 and 90 day unless you test it, and find your market to respond better to the 30, 60, 90 day program.

So after you decide which program you're going to use, then you need to decide on what you're going to send them. Postcards or letters.

I used the postcards for several years because they were cheaper to mail. At the time, postage to mail a postcard was .27 each, and the postcard cost me .17 each, for a total of .44 per customer.

The postcards pulled me in a response rate of 10.66%. Not too shabby of a response rate.

However, when I wrote a personal letter to these same people, my response rate jumped to 21.95%! That's more than a double the response that the postcards got!

Now it did cost me .50 to mail out a letter, vs. the .44 to mail out the postcard, but the difference in the response rate certainly made it more profitable to mail out the letter.

Once again, letters are much more personal than a postcard. I would recommend testing both in your market, but I'm almost positive the personal letter will out produce the postcard every time.

Figure 6:1 is a copy of the actual letter that I would send to my 45 day lazy customers. Once you have your letter written and saved in your computer, it doesn't take any time to print them out as you need them and sign them in blue ink.

Notice how many times the word **FREE** is used, even though they are actually only getting one item for free.

The P.P.S at the bottom wasn't always on this letter. That's a reminder for the customer to sign up for our texting club. Once again, notice how many times **FREE** is used.

Figure 6:1

This FREE calizone is for YOU!

Dear neighbor,

Hi, my name is Paul. I'm the owner of the Simple Simon Pizza right here in Pryor.

A few days ago I was looking thru my list of customers and noticed that you haven't called us in a while. So to entice you back, I want to give you a **FREE** calizone!

That's right – I'll give you a **FREE** calizone when you buy any large pizza at menu price, and I'll even deliver it – **FREE!**

I know how hectic things can get around this time of year – so why spend all that time cooking and cleaning when you can treat your family to a **FREE** calizone, stuffed with over half a pound of meats and cheeses and cooked to a golden brown.

You'll get enough food to feed your entire family – and for a lot less than you would have spent for just one pizza at those big corporate pizza stores.

Plus – I always put my neck on the line with every order – If you should ever be disappointed – for any reason, please let me know. If I cant make it right – I'll give you your money back – every penny!

Give us a call now! You'll get fast **FREE** delivery right to your front door, or you can pick up. You'll find us at 125 Steve Berry Blvd, right across the street from Wal Mart. Our phone number is **825-5500**

Hope to see you again soon,

Paul Baker

P.S. Please – take me up on this offer tonight! But definitely before this letter expires. The **FREE** calizone and **FREE** delivery are yours – and as always – if you're not 100% satisfied, your money back – every penny!

P.P.S. Be sure to sign up for our text coupons by texting the word **SSPPRYOR** to **74700.** You'll immediately receive a coupon for a **FREE** fountain drink –PLUS – a chance to win a **FREE** large pizza of your choice. You'll also receive coupons by text for **FREE** pizzas, **FREE** calizones, and **FREE** cheesesticks!

This letter expires on **06/11/09**

Upselling

Chapter 7

M ost pizzerias can expect to make anywhere from an additional $2000- $24,000 per year by upselling. How much you can make depends on how consistent you are with your upselling and if you use the correct upselling techniques.

Yes, there are correct techniques that will make upselling easy and painless, and your customers won't even know their being upsold.

Let's look at how most places try to upsell.

McDonalds always upsells when you go through the drive thru. You have probably experienced this yourself. You get done placing your order and the person on the intercom then asks you "would you like to try an apple pie with your order today?"

Obviously, no… If I wanted an apple pie, I would have asked for one. I'm sure they sell a few pies this way, but there's a better way as we'll soon see.

Let's look into the psychology of buying real quickly so we can understand why these techniques work.

Your brain is divided into two parts – the right side and the left side. The right side is the emotional half, the left side is the analytical, or logical half. I would venture to say that 99% of all buying is done by the right side (emotional) of the brain.

If you were to ask someone which side of their brain they used when making a buying decision, they would almost always tell you they used the logical left side and not the emotional right to make their buying decision.

But that is completely untrue. When someone buys a new car, they will tell you that they purchased it because it gets great gas mileage, or because they got a good deal on it, or because they needed a car with more room.

But truth be told, if you were to offer them a butt ugly car with just plain interior, and no bells or whistles, they wouldn't buy it, even if it was a better deal, got better gas mileage, and had more room than the car they bought. If they were buying off of pure logic, they would pick the second car.

But they don't buy off of logic, they buy off of emotion. Emotions will affect what people buy. Just look at toilet paper. Why do you think they put a picture of a baby surrounded by soft linens on the packaging of toilet paper?

Buying is an emotional decision, and when people go to buy, they get into what's known as a buying mode.

How many times have you gone in to an electronics or retail store to buy a new television, and come out not only with a new television, but a new dvd player, new surround sound, and some other funky looking gadget that you're not sure what exactly it does, but it looks really cool with your new TV?

This usually happens because you get into a buying mode. People like to buy, they hate to be sold.

When people are in your pizzeria, they are in a spending mode and want to buy. It's your job not to disrupt that mode.

How do we do that? The absolute best way I've found is to use the technique created by Kamron Karington (I highly recommend you read his book Gun To The Head Marketing). Using the technique he has created you're essentially asking for the upsale... without asking. That might sound kind of confusing but let's try to explain it by taking another look at our trip through the McDonalds drive thru.

You've just pulled up to the menu board, you've had to take an hour late lunch, so you're starving and could eat almost anything even... McDonalds. You look at the menu board and tell yourself you want the cheeseburger and fries. Then you decide to make it a double meat cheeseburger, and what the heck, lets super size the fries… gotta make up for that late lunch, and what the heck, might as well get a large coke while you're there.

You decide to buy all this in less than 15 seconds because you're in a buying mode. You didn't stop to think if you could even finish eating a double meat cheese burger with a super sized French fry and large soda.

Now after you place your order, our friendly McDonalds employee at the other end of the intercom asks you the "Would you like to try an apple pie with your order today?"

At that point, now your brain is asking yourself "Do I want an apple pie?" "Do I even like apple pie?" "How much is it?" "I hate it when someone tries to sell me something, if I had wanted an apple pie, I would have ordered an apple pie!" So you tell the order taker "No thanks."

By asking you a question, the order taker interrupted your buying mode. You had to stop and think about what he was asking you and make a decision. So you shifted from the emotional right side of the brain, to the analytical left side that contemplates the question being asked and makes a decision.

So now our left side of the brain is in control, and it realizes that someone is trying to sell us something, so we throw up our defenses. Did you notice that? In that 15 second period, I was "buying" when the order taker asked me if I wanted a pie, I was now being sold to.

What we're going to do when we upsell is sneak past those defenses, and keep the customer in the buying mode using the emotional side of their brain.

So how do we do it?

Let's look once again at our little trip through the drive through. You're in the middle of giving your order...

"Hi, I'd like a large coke, a double meat cheeseburger...

Right then and there the order taker says in an assuming voice... "extra cheese on that?" And you say "Sure, and a large order of fries too."

Did you catch that little trick? Kameron hit the nail on the head when he coined the "extra cheese on that" phrase. It works perfectly to ask for the upsale without breaking the customers buying mode.

Using this one technique alone brought me in on average $3700 per year in additional free money.

Why does this work?

By just slipping in the "extra cheese on that" you're not disrupting the buying mode that the customer is in.

When you say the phrase, you want to say it in an assuming voice and pitch so it sounds like you're assuming that since everyone else gets extra cheese, you'll naturally want extra cheese too.

Now if you were to say "Do you want extra cheese on that" or "Would you like extra cheese on that" then you're asking a question and interrupting the buying process. Now the customer has to stop and think if they want extra cheese.

You have just switched them from the emotional right to the logical left side of the brain.

This strategy works on almost any item.

Bacon Cheese Burger – "extra bacon on that"

Seafood Alfredo Pasta – "extra shrimp in that"

Eggs, Sausage and Biscuit breakfast – "extra sausage with that"

Look through your menu and see what you can have your staff upsell on. Be careful of trying to upsell something that isn't relative to what the customer is already buying. You obviously wouldn't want to try to upsell extra cheese on an order of cinnamon sticks.

So now that you've upsold your customers on extra cheese, or toppings we want to take it one step farther. After you've taken your customers order you will want to upsell them again on an item that they didn't already order.

I always had my staff upsell them on a calizone or a large order of cheese sticks if they didn't order one of those two items. These two upsells we're steeply discounted to get the sale. The calizone usually sold for $9.99 but it was offered as an add on for $5 dollars. The large cheese sticks normally sold for $5.99 and we upsold them for $2.99. You can call these addons "managers specials" or "daily specials" doesn't really matter, just make sure your staff is upselling them.

This did raise our food costs but that's ok, and here's why.

If you sold a large one topping pizza for 10 bucks, and subtract 30% food cost your left with $7.00 that will be deposited into your bank account.

Now if you add on a calizone to this same order for $5.00 with a food cost of 50%, you're going to be depositing $9.50 in your bank account for the transaction.

Which would you much rather deposit into your bank account, $7.00 or $9.50? I'll make $9.50 deposits all day long with my food cost being 40% over making a $7.00 deposit with 30% food cost.

On average I found that if my staff upsold consistently like they were supposed to, we could upsell 20% to 30% of our orders. So with our $25,000 example pizzeria, if we only managed to upsell the cheese sticks on just 20% of the orders we're still looking at potentially making an additional $750 per month or $9,000 per year.

Upselling really is free money. You just have to ask for it.

Using Image Advertising Instead of Direct Response Advertising

Chapter 8

C ountless billions have been wasted on what's known as "image advertising." Yes, that's billions with a big fat "B". It appears that no industry is immune to using image advertising and that includes pizzerias.

Most pizzeria owners know that they need to advertise in some way, shape or form. The problem is, we all (yes me included) have done the worst kind of advertising that you can do and that's image advertising. Using image advertising when you're barely making ends meet will bankrupt you fast.

But before I go any further, I had better back up because at this point you might be asking "What the heck is image advertising"? The picture in figure 8:1 is a perfect example of image advertising.

Image advertising is what I would refer to as name, rank and serial number advertising. It's where you basically put your name, phone number, address and maybe some goofy slogan like "we're the best" out there and hope that someone buys a pizza because of it. This type of advertising is so bad it's even been referred to as "tombstone" advertising. Because well... it looks like what you would put on a tombstone, and if you continue to spend your money advertising this way your business will be dead in no time.

These types of advertisements rarely ever work and yet everyone uses them. Look through the yellow pages in your phone book. The yellow pages are filled with examples of name, rank, serial number advertising.

Figure 8:1

Ever been watching a football or baseball game and in the background you see some company's logo in the background? It's usually a big name brand like Budweiser, McDonalds,

Pepsi, Coke or Nike. This is another good example of image advertising.

Fortunately for these gigantic companies, they can afford to pay out the millions of dollars every year to have their logo plastered somewhere. You don't, and to think that you can spend your advertising dollars on displaying your logo and phone number like these huge companies and stay in business for very long is insanity.

Your logo, as pretty as it may be, is not going to entice people to call you and order pizza, and actually your logo is the last thing you should be worried about when advertising your pizzeria.

Look – you need a way to distinguish yourself from other businesses so your customers know who to call and your name and logo do just that. But it should in no way be the front and center of your marketing and advertising. Why not? Here's the honest truth, and it might hurt a bit... Because your customers don't care what your logo looks like.

I know a lot of folks may point at the big companies and say "look, they use their logo as advertising and they have a lot of money and they're not dumb." Well... yes they have a lot of money and the "not dumb" is debatable. Those big companies are more interested in making their shareholders and board of directors happy than using advertising that pulls in sales.

The first year I had my pizza restaurant I used image advertising exclusively. I didn't know any better. It was what every other business used so I figured it must work. It was a big financial mistake. Here's some of my failures using image based advertising.

Within a few weeks after buying my store, the newspaper ad rep showed up and "convinced" me to place a business card size ad in the local paper. The ad rep told me all I needed to do was give her one of my business cards, $250 bucks and she would do the rest. What a deal huh! What did the ad look like? Yep, Name rank and serial number format. It was my stores logo and phone number pasted in black and white for the whole town to see.

A few months later, another sales rep came in promoting some kind of stupid "boom stick" advertising for the local football team. These were some kind of goofy inflatable sticks that the fans could beat together at the football games to make noise. I could put my logo and phone number on these things and the people who bought them to "make noise" at the football games would get $2 off any large pizza if they brought their boom sticks in to my restaurant. This was dumb of me to buy into this on so many levels. How much did this wonderful type of advertising cost me? Only $650 to get my logo on 50 boom sticks.

Valentine's Day comes along. Same newspaper sales rep tells me they have a "special" Valentine's Day issues coming out. Because this is a special issue, I can advertise for only $200 this time. Once again, she just needs a business card and $200 bucks to make this happen. Newspaper comes out and the ad looks strangely like the last one did, with the exception of having a bunch of goofy "hearts" all over the ad. When I looked through the newspaper there were about 20 other ads with the exact same format, a basic business card with stupid hearts all over them.

After these failures I decided to get serious. I had a local printing company print up 5000 postcards in black and white with a $1.00 off coupon on them. The headline read "We want your business!" Then I had them put my logo as big as I could get it right in the middle of the postcard with a picture of a pizza crammed in there as well. This work of art is obviously going to kick some ass… right?

I had exactly one coupon redeemed. It was the crackheads that lived across the street in a garage. These folks didn't have a car and ordered from us every couple of days anyways because we were the only ones that were within walking distance for them. So technically by them redeeming the postcard I actually shorted myself a dollar off the pizza that I would have normally gotten full price for. This wonderful mail campaign only cost me $1,450.

That same month I had a salesman come in and sell me advertising in some kind of newborn baby book. This book is basically something that the hospital gives out to new mothers. It has the baby's picture, weight, length, how many times they pooped or pissed in the first hour of being born, that kind of stuff. I was told that this book would be very sentimental to the parents and would be kept for a lifetime, and for a mere $500 dollars I could have my business card sized ad placed in the back. He just needed a copy of my business card, $500 dollars and he would take care of the rest.

So let's stop here before I divulge any more of my abysmal failures and see how much money I wasted within 6 months. When we add it all up, it comes to ... $3,050 flushed down the toilet, and at a time when I didn't have any money to waste. Oh sure, it "got my name out there" but didn't bring me anything back in sales.

So why do so many pizzeria owners use this type of advertising? There are two main answers to this question.

The first and most common reason is they simply don't know any better. They look at what everyone else is doing for advertising and marketing in the pizza industry and then copy that. This is what I refer to as "marketing incest" because just like real incest, the longer it goes on, the stupider everyone gets.

Pizzeria A copies what Pizzeria B is doing, which is copying what Pizzeria C is doing, which originally got the idea from Pizzeria A. It's a viscous never ending cycle.

The second reason that people use image advertising is because that's the type of advertising that's sold to them. Image advertising is great for the salespeople selling the ad space because they get paid for selling the ad, not for the results you get from the ad. How many of these ad businesses would stay in business if they had to guarantee results? Do you think you would ever hear one of these salesmen tell you to place the ad, then only pay them based on how many people responded to the ad?

Ad salesmen love image advertising because they can't be held accountable when the ad fails. They can blame it on the economy or it seems like their favorite excuse is "you didn't run the ad enough times." This is incompetence at its highest level. A direct response ad will work the first time, and if it doesn't, you don't run it a second time. Lots of advertising sales reps will try to lock you into a yearly contract depending on what kind of media you are using to advertise. They will probably give you some kind of discount if you agree to place your ad 12 times in the next year. The problem with this is – if your ad didn't work the first time, why the hell do you think it will work on the eleventh or twelfth time it runs? They will give you the "You need to get your name out there and run the ad multiple times to get exposure" line of crap. Well guess what... people die from exposure!

I see so many businesses (not just pizzerias) running the same image ads over and over and over again, knowing there is no possible way that ad is even getting close to paying for itself.

Here's the truth, the ad salesmen that contacts you to sell you ad space in any format are only there to sell the ad space, they have no idea how to create an advertisement or marketing campaign that gets results.

So now that I've beaten up on the ad salesmen a bit, let me state that it's not entirely their fault the ad doesn't work. It's yours!

You're the one paying for the ad, you're the one who should create the ad. You should never, ever, let the ad salesmen create your advertisement. Ad salesmen are akin to yellow belts in karate. They have just enough knowledge to make them cocky but would get their asses kicked if they showed up at a biker bar. So you have to take responsibility of what goes on your advertisement.

At this point I might have scared you from advertising altogether and I hope that's not the case, because there is a type of marketing that you should be using consistently in your pizzeria. That type of marketing is what's known as "direct response marketing," and unlike image advertising, it can potentially make you very rich. What is direct response marketing? Simply put, its marketing and advertising that gets a response.

When you put out a direct response advertisement, you get a response back from your customers, and the response isn't months later, its immediate.

Think back to the last time you put out an image ad. Did your phones ring off the hook, or were you checking them to make sure they were still working because business was so slow? Direct response marketing works, and it works fast. In my own experience with using direct response marketing I grew my sales 233%.

Keep this in mind as well. It doesn't cost you any more to place a direct response style ad instead of an image ad. The only real difference is the message. Reach into your pocket right now and pull out a $1 dollar bill and a $100 dollar bill. Place them both in front of you and look closely at them. What's the difference? The message! They are both made out of the same paper, cut the same size, have the same ink, but the message on one only makes it worth $1 while the message on the other makes it worth $100.

Here are the components of a direct response advertisement. A good advertisement will have all of these in it.

1. A headline

2. Creates interest in your pizza

3. Creates desire in your prospective customer

4. Has a specific offer

5. Has a deadline to respond or a cut off date

Let's take a look at each of these components individually.

Headline:
Every ad you ever put out absolutely must, with no exception have a headline. It doesn't matter if you sending out something as simple as a postcard or tattooing your advertisement on a strippers butt cheek (from what I hear you

can actually do that now) everything you do will have a headline.

If you've ever gone through a newspaper you've probably noticed that above each article there's a headline. This lets the reader know what the article is about. Have you ever read every single article in a newspaper? Probably not, most likely you scanned the headlines, and then read the articles that you were interested in. If you are a sports enthusiast and seen a headline that said...

"Dallas Cowboy Football Team Beats The Crap Out Of Franchise Owner Jimmy Johnson After Another Staggering Loss!"

Would that catch your attention if you liked sports? Probably, then you would go on to read the article. Now what if you're going through the newspaper and you come across a headline that read...

"New Design In Women's Summer Dresses Creating Big Buzz At New York Fashion Show"

You being a sports fanatic and seeing this headline are probably not going to go and read this article. And if you do, you probably more issues there than I care to address.

Now imagine this same newspaper, but it doesn't have a single headline anywhere. Not a one. It's just the articles. How would you know which article that you might be interested in reading about? You wouldn't know. You would

63

have to read each article to see what is was about. That's just not going to happen in this busy world. You would toss the newspaper without a second thought.

Do you see how important a headline is? Your headline calls out to the people who are interested in what you have and it absolutely must reach out and grab your potential customer and make them want to read more.

Creates Interest:

Your advertisement has to be interesting. Once again, you can't expect your name and logo to do this. You cannot bore someone into buying a pizza from you.

Creates Desire:

After your ad has caught their attention, and got them interested, then you need to make them "desire" your pizza. Use lots of descriptive words, paint a picture in their mind about what they will experience. Which of these makes you desire the pizza more...

"Large pizzas delivered to your house hot a fast for $9.99."

Or...

"Your pizza will arrive at your front door in less than 30 minute, piping hot, piled with your favorite toppings and smothered in over half of pound aged mozzarella cheese for less than you would pay for one of those corporate chain store pizzas."

Does the second one make you desire a pizza a bit more?

Specific Offer:
The worst offer you can make in your ads is no offer at all. The next worst offer you can make is a crappy dollar off offer. Yes, it's better than no offer at all, but don't expect people to beat down your door to buy a pizza from you with a $2 off coupon.

Remember in the Godfather movie when Marlon Brando said "I'm gonna make them an offer they can't refuse." That's what kind of offer you need to make – a mafia offer. It has to be so good and so convincing that your prospective customer can't help but take you up on it.

Instead of price discounting or dollar off coupons, I've always done free items. One of the better offers that I had was either a free calizone or free medium pizza when you purchased a large pizza. Both the calizone and medium pizza would cost me around $1.89 to give away free, but had a value to the customer of $9.99.

You'll get a big difference in response just by giving away something with a high perceived value over a limp dollar off coupon. And from my experiences, the more free items you pack on to your offer, the more response you'll get. Three items seems to be the "magic number" in response. Try giving away free breadsticks, free 2liter and free delivery with any large pizza. Those are all low cost items for the owners, but the customer puts a huge value on them.
Never put out an ad without an offer.

Having a Deadline:

Your direct response ads must have a deadline or cutoff date for the offer. Everyone procrastinates, and by not putting a deadline on your offer you're giving them permission to procrastinate. We all know what really happens when we procrastinate – it never happens. Your potential customers are much more likely to call you if they know that the offer ends on a specific date and that they will miss out if they don't call by then. And besides, without an expiration date or deadline, you run the risk of someone wanting that offer months, maybe even years after you ran the ad for it.

So now that you know what the key components are for creating a direct response advertisement, there only one more thing you must do.

Track your results. From now on, every advertisement or marketing campaign that you do must be tracked. Without tracking your results, you really don't have a clue if your advertisement brought you in a profit or a loss. Once again, a Point of Sale system will save you tons of time and make things extremely easy when it comes to tracking your ads.

I've lost track of how many people have told me they have a great looking ad in a newspaper, on a flier, or on a Valpak coupon that when asked, can't tell me what their results are. They really have no clue how much money the advertisement has made or lost for them.

They usually "think" it's working well but really don't know. From now on track everything you put out.

Final Thoughts

Chapter 9

If you have come to the end of this book and are already doing all seven things in your pizzeria, then I tip my hat to you and give you a big congratulations. You're definitely on top of your game and are most than likely doing much better than your competitors are.

However, if you have reached the end of this book and now realize that you are not doing some or all of the seven things, then I encourage you to "buckle down" and get things done. You might be tempted to ignore some of these things because they are "overly simple" but remember – little hinges swing big doors.

So let's take one final look at our $25,000 per month example pizzeria and see how things add up.

In chapter one you discovered why you need to raise your prices. By raising prices 10% we've instantly raised sales by $30,000 per year.

In chapter two you learned why you need to start using direct mail even though it's more expensive than social media. By using a direct mail campaign to acquire and attract new repeat customers you could potentially add an additional $41,472 per year.

In chapter three we talked about how important portion control is. By creating portion control charts and having your employees build all their pizzas to those charts you are keeping an additional $10,350 in your pocket every year just in cheese alone.

Chapter four we looked at why a point of sale system is one of the most important pieces of equipment you can have in your pizzeria. There's no way to guess on a dollar amount that you might be losing due to theft so we won't figure that in, but keep in mind that more than likely there is some kind of theft going on in your pizzeria right now.

By using your point of sale system to monitor your labor, you can now prevent overshooting your projected labor percentage cutting your payroll by $15,000 per year.

Chapter five we learned about customer retention. By implementing a lazy customer program we found out how we could keep our customers from "forgetting about us" and wondering off to a competitor.

Chapter 6 we covered upselling. By consistently having our staff upsell extra cheese and other additional items we're looking at potentially adding an extra $9,000 per year.

Chapter 7 we discovered why we don't ever want to use image advertising and why we never ever want to allow an ad sales rep to create our ads for us.

The dollar amount on our $25,000 example pizzeria is $105,822. How long do you think this pizzeria would last bleeding out that much money year after year?

But the real question you need to ask yourself is how long can you last bleeding out this much money?

Bonus Chapter
The Million Dollar
Question

Chapter 10

W hat kind of business are you in? When you ask any business owner that question the inevitable response is always something like "I'm in the restaurant business" or "I'm in the car business" or "I'm in the insurance business" or for pizzeria owners its usually "I'm in the pizza business."

While these answers are "technically" correct, it shows the mindset of the owners in their respective industries. What I'm going to attempt to reveal to you in this bonus chapter is a different way to look at your business. A different way that if you really "get it" and understand it, it could quickly create a million dollar pizza business for you. I know this might be difficult for you to grasp at first, but let me try explaining it with a few examples.

Ray Crock founder of McDonalds once asked some college students "What business do you think I'm in?" The college students chuckled thinking he was joking. He asked them again "What kind of business do you think I'm in?"

The college students still thinking he was joking with them said "Ray, we all know you're in the hamburger business". Ray promptly told them they were wrong.

First and foremost he told them "I'm in the marketing business" second, he said "I'm in the real estate business" and lastly "I'm in the hamburger business".

Isn't that kind of strange that the guy who created McDonalds and has sold billions of hamburgers all over the world wouldn't think of his business as being first and foremost in the hamburger business? Ray Crock knew that there were thousands of other burger and fry places out there that were in the "hamburger" business so he went into the "marketing" business first and foremost. Then he went into the real estate business. Have you ever noticed that with very few exceptions McDonalds restaurants are always located on prime real estate in heavy traffic areas? Usually these locations themselves are worth a small fortune, so even if McDonalds didn't sell a billion hamburgers, the real estate that they sit on is still worth millions to the company. Do you see how Ray Crock had a different way of looking at what kind of business he was in?

Here's another example. In the 1940s Amusement parks were considered "shady" places to take your family to.

Drinking of alcohol was permitted, employees looked like cigar chomping thugs, and rigged games we're the norm. Walt Disney was disgusted by what he saw at these parks so instead of building another amusement park, he created "the happiest place on earth."

Walt Disney was not in the amusement park business, or the movie business, or the cartoon business. Walt Disney was in the "making people happy business." Do you think Disney would have grown into the Empire today if Walt had only thought of his business as another amusement park?

You can find this kind of thinking in almost all highly successful businesses. Look at professional wrestling for another example. Vince McMahon owner of World Wrestling Entertainment was doing an interview for a cable news channel. He was telling the story about how another businessman that he knew had started a new wrestling franchise. This businessman had called Vince up and told him "Hey Vince, guess what... I'm in the wrestling business!" To which Vince responded, "That's great, at least we're not competitors because I'm not in the wrestling business, I'm in the entertainment business."

Vince McMahon knew what kind of business he was in. He was in the entertainment business, not the wrestling business. Oh, and the new wrestling franchise that was started by this businessman... didn't last but a few years.

Are you beginning to see why you can't just view yourself as being in the pizza business? When you shift paradigms and begin looking at your pizza business in a different way, the results can be spectacular. When this way of thinking finally "clicked" for me, I began not thinking of myself as being in the pizza business, but instead as a being a marketing business that sells pizza.

Did that just cause an "aha" moment? I hope so. Do you see how differently you look at your business when you think you're a marketing business that sells pizza? Everything changes now.

Pizza Success Secrets

**The author, Paul Baker
is available for individual consulting
schedule permitting.**

**You may contact him by email at
paul@blackopspizzamarketing.com**

Made in the USA
Monee, IL
24 July 2021

74211960R00046